I Love My Pet
RABBIT

Aaron Carr

Go to **www.av2books.com**, and enter this book's unique code.

BOOK CODE

L634378

AV² by Weigl brings you media enhanced books that support active learning.

AV² provides enriched content that supplements and complements this book. Weigl's AV² books strive to create inspired learning and engage young minds in a total learning experience.

Your AV² Media Enhanced books come alive with...

 Audio
Listen to sections of the book read aloud.

 Video
Watch informative video clips.

 Embedded Weblinks
Gain additional information for research.

 Try This!
Complete activities and hands-on experiments.

 Key Words
Study vocabulary, and complete a matching word activity.

 Quizzes
Test your knowledge.

 Slide Show
View images and captions, and prepare a presentation.

... and much, much more!

Published by AV² by Weigl
350 5th Avenue, 59th Floor New York, NY 10118
Website: www.av2books.com www.weigl.com

Library of Congress Cataloging-in-Publication Data

Carr, Aaron.
 Rabbit / Aaron Carr.
   p. cm. -- (I love my pet)
 ISBN 978-1-61690-924-6 (hardcover : alk. paper) -- ISBN 978-1-61690-570-5 (online)
 1. Rabbits--Juvenile literature. I. Title.
 SF453.2.C37 2012
 636.932'2--dc23

                          2011025203
Printed in the United States of America in North Mankato, Minnesota
1 2 3 4 5 6 7 8 9 0 15 14 13 12 11

062011
WEP030611

Project Coordinator: Aaron Carr   Art Director: Terry Paulhus
Weigl acknowledges Getty Images, iStock, and Dreamstime as image suppliers for this title.

I Love My Pet
RABBIT

CONTENTS

2 AV² Book Code

4 Rabbit

6 Life Cycle

10 Features

14 Care

20 Health

22 Rabbit Facts

24 Word List

24 www.av2books.com

3

I love my pet rabbit.
I take good care of her.

5

My pet rabbit was a kitten.
She did not have any fur.

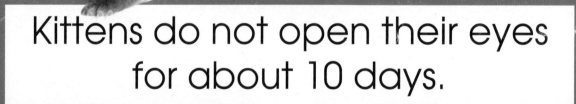

Kittens do not open their eyes
for about 10 days.

My pet rabbit was little when I took her home. She was eight weeks old.

My pet rabbit has big ears.
She uses her ears to cool off.

My pet rabbit
moves her nose very fast.
This helps her to smell.

A rabbit can wiggle its nose
up to 120 times a minute.

13

My pet rabbit
sleeps 11 hours each day.
She sleeps most of the day.

Some rabbits sleep
with their eyes open.

My pet rabbit
only eats once a day.
I give her food
every morning.

My pet rabbit
needs to be brushed often.
Her nails must also be cut.

19

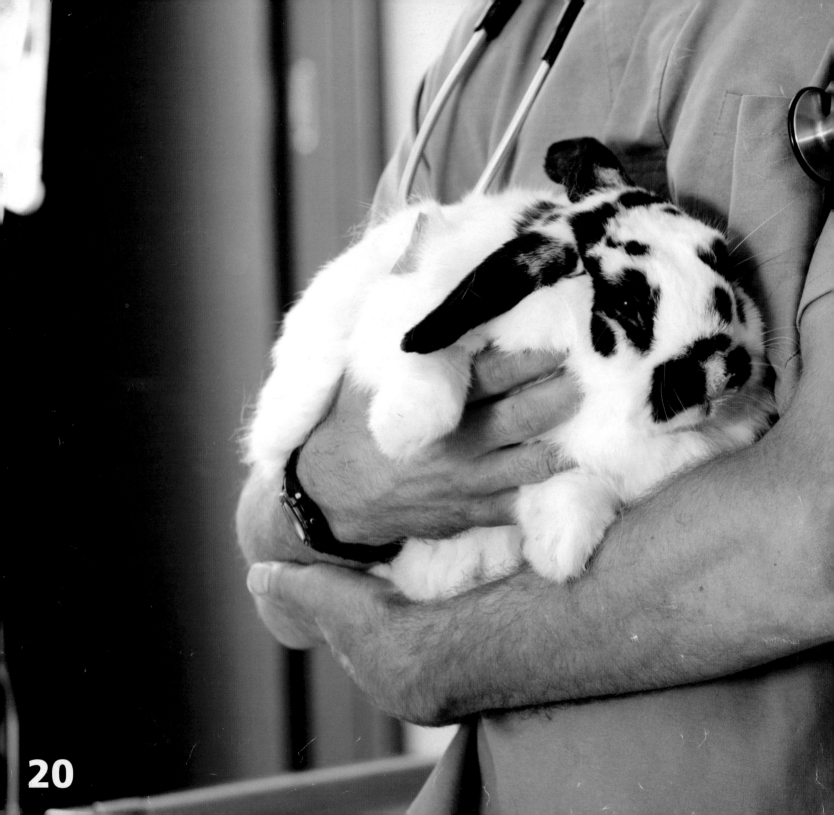

I help make sure
my pet rabbit is healthy.
I love my pet rabbit.

RABBIT FACTS

This page provides more detail about the interesting facts found in the book.
Simply look for the corresponding page number to match the fact.

Pages 4-5

I love my pet rabbit. I take good care of her. More than 12 million rabbits are raised in the United States each year. Rabbits make great pets because they are clean, smart, and quiet. Keeping a rabbit for a pet is a big responsibility. Rabbits can live between eight and 10 years. They need regular care throughout that time.

Pages 6–7

My pet rabbit was a kitten. She did not have any fur. Baby rabbits are called kittens. Newborn kittens do not have fur, and their eyes are closed for several days. Never handle a newborn kitten. By about five weeks of age, kittens begin to explore. Their fur has grown, and their eyes are open. Kittens can be picked up after three weeks of age.

Pages 8–9

My pet rabbit was little when I took her home. She was eight weeks old. By eight to 10 weeks of age, rabbits can be separated from their mother to go to a new home. Never take a rabbit from its mother until it is at least eight weeks old. Most rabbits are full grown by six months of age. They require plenty of exercise and attention.

Pages 10–11

My pet rabbit has big, floppy ears. She uses her ears to stay cool. A rabbit's big, floppy ears help it hear sounds from all directions. Rabbits also use their ears to stay cool in hot temperatures. Rabbits have blood vessels in their ears that help keep them cool when they get too hot.

Pages 12–13

My pet rabbit moves her nose very fast. This helps her to smell. Rabbits have an excellent sense of smell. Your pet rabbit may twitch her nose between 20 and 120 times in one minute. This helps her detect more smells. In nature, rabbits rely on their senses of smell and hearing to detect danger.

Pages 14–15

My pet rabbit sleeps 11 hours a day. She sleeps most of the day. Rabbits are crepuscular. This means they sleep most during the evening and early morning and are most active at night. Rabbits often sleep with their eyes open. Do not worry if you see your pet rabbit sleeping with her eyes open. This is perfectly normal.

Pages 16–17

My pet rabbit only eats once a day. I feed her every morning. Rabbits only need to eat once or twice a day. Rabbits only eat plant matter. A mix of store-bought rabbit pellets and fresh fruits and vegetables will provide a healthy diet. Rabbits also need to eat plenty of hay, which helps them with digestion.

Pages 18–19

My pet rabbit needs to be brushed often. Her nails must also be cut. Rabbits can get hairballs if they swallow too much fur while grooming. Brushing your rabbit often can help prevent hairballs. Rabbits also need their nails cut on a regular basis. Ask a veterinarian to show you how to properly clip your rabbit's nails.

Pages 20–21

I help my pet rabbit stay healthy. I love my pet rabbit. To keep your rabbit healthy and happy, feed her at the same time every day, brush her fur and clip her nails regularly, and clean her hutch two or three times a week. Stress can cause rabbits to become sick. Place your rabbit's hutch in a safe place away from other animals, loud noises, direct sunlight, and damp conditions.

WORD LIST

Research has shown that as much as 65 percent of all written material published in English is made up of 300 words. These 300 words cannot be taught using pictures or learned by sounding them out. They must be recognized by sight. This book contains 59 common sight words to help young readers improve their reading fluency and comprehension. This book also teaches young readers several important content words, such as proper nouns. These words are paired with pictures to aid in learning and improve understanding.

Page	Sight Words First Appearance	Page	Content Words First Appearance
4	good, her, I, my, of, take	4	pet, rabbit
6	a, about, any, days, did, do, eyes, for, have, not, open, she, their, was	6	fur, kitten
		9	home, weeks
9	home, little, old, took, when	11	ears
11	big, has, off, to, uses	12	minute, nose
12	can, helps, moves, this, times, up, very	17	morning
15	each, hours, most, open, some, the, their, with	18	nails
17	eats, every, food, give, once, only		
18	also, be, cut, must, needs, often		
21	is, make		

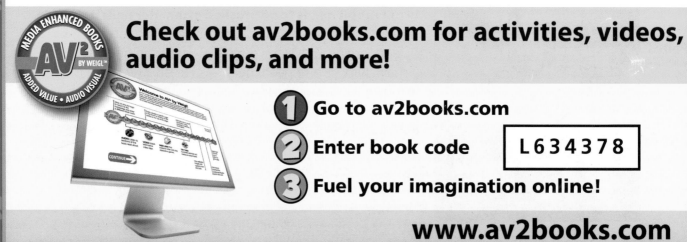

Check out av2books.com for activities, videos, audio clips, and more!

1 Go to av2books.com

2 Enter book code   L 6 3 4 3 7 8

3 Fuel your imagination online!

www.av2books.com

24